T0197590

Our Family's Faith

BY

Judy Francis

ILLUSTRATED BY

WESTBOW PRESS

WestBow Press books may be ordered through booksellers or by contacting:

WestBow Press
A Division of Thomas Nelson & Zondervan
1663 Liberty Drive
Bloomington, IN 47403
www.westbowpress.com
1 (866) 928-1240

ISBN: 978-1-4908-8595-7 (sc)
ISBN: 978-1-4908-8596-4 (e)

Library of Congress Control Number: 2015910130

Print information available on the last page.

WestBow Press rev. date: 12/28/2015

WESTBOW
PRESS®
A DIVISION OF THOMAS NELSON
& ZONDERVAN

GIFT TO: _____

_____

FROM:

_____

_____

_____

DATE/NOTE:

_____
_____
_____
_____
_____
_____
_____
_____
_____
_____
_____
_____
_____
_____
_____
_____
_____
_____

"Seek God first and His righteousness and all shall be added to you." (Matthew 6:33)

"I can do all things through Christ who strengthens me." (Philippians 4:13)

Dedicated with love and affection to my family –
Aisha, Clayton, and Christopher,

in honor of our ancestors.

As for me and my household, we will serve the Lord.
(Joshua 24:15)

2

Our family starts each day reading the Bible and praising God for all our blessings –

food to eat, clothes to wear, shelter from all storms, and love for one another.

God gave us the sun to greet us daily so we can enjoy walking and watching –

red birds in flight, butterflies floating across the trail, lady bugs strolling through the forest,

flowers bending to and fro with the rhythm of the wind,

and then --

God gave us the evening sunset to calm our busy day of work and play –

we end our day thinking about every good moment sent our way –

with a small still voice leading us to "always" do the right thing –

we also think about the things that went wrong,

asking God's forgiveness, and seeking God's help to avoid the same mistakes.

Our family ends each night kneeling and reciting –

THE LORD'S PRAYER

Our Father, who art in heaven, hollowed be Thy name. Thy kingdom come. Thy will be done on earth, as it is in heaven.

Give us this day our daily bread, and forgive us our trespasses, as we forgive those who trespass against us.

And lead us not into temptation, but deliver us from evil.

Amen. (Matthew 6:9-13)

--and then, we fall asleep, resting under God's care.

RECORD YOUR FAMILY TRADITIONS OF FAITH

_____
_____
_____
_____
_____
_____
_____
_____
_____
_____
_____
_____
_____
_____
_____
_____
_____
_____
_____
_____
_____
_____
_____

For He gave His laws—and commanded parents to teach them to their children, so that they in turn could teach their children too. Thus His laws pass down from generation to generation. (Psalms 78:5-6)

ABOUT THE AUTHOR

Judy (Turner) Francis, a former insurance manager with a Fortune 500 company, always dreamed of writing Christian children's books as her encore career. This is the first book of her inspired series. She was born and raised in Nashville, Tennessee; received her B. A. degree from Spelman College and attended the Atlanta University School of Public Administration. She currently resides in the Wilmington, North Carolina area.

This book is a personal conveyance of her love and respect for Christian family values, as captured by brilliant illustrations of family traditions.

Printed in the United States
by Baker & Taylor Publisher Services